Masonic Funeral Prayer Book

Elijah Abner

DEDICATION

This book is dedicated to the builders and safe keepers of the craft. May it bring light to your darkness, comfort to your troubled soul, and compassion to your weary heart while on your masonic journey. Let us keep the memories of our departed brethren in our hearts till we meet again in that Celestial Lodge above.

CONTENTS

Know Thyself

The Quiet Journey Home

Dear Great Architect of the Universe,

We gather here today to mourn the passing of our beloved brother, who has completed his journey in this earthly life and now embarks on his quiet journey home.

As a faithful Freemason, he has lived a life of honor and service, and his legacy will continue to inspire and guide us in our own journeys.

We pray for comfort and peace for his family and friends, as they come to terms with their loss. May they find solace in the memories they shared with our departed brother, and in the knowledge that he has now joined the great lodge above.

We also pray for our brother's safe and peaceful passage to the Grand Lodge above, where we trust he will find eternal rest in the presence of the Great Architect of the Universe.

May his spirit be received with open arms by those who have gone before him, and may he be greeted with the words, "Well done, good and faithful servant."

We offer our heartfelt thanks for the blessings our brother brought to our lives, and for the gift of his quiet journey home.

In the name of the Great Architect of the Universe, we pray. Amen.

The Guiding Light

Great Architect of the Universe,

We come before you today to honor and bid farewell to our beloved brother, a guiding light in the world of Freemasonry. We thank you for the gift of his leadership, wisdom, and example that have inspired countless brothers and sisters in the Masonic fraternity.

As we mourn his passing, we also give thanks for the many years we were privileged to share with him, for the countless lives he touched, and the lessons he imparted.

We ask for comfort and strength for his family and friends, as they grieve and seek to make sense of this loss. May they be comforted by the knowledge that his legacy will continue to inspire and guide us all, as we walk in the path that he has illuminated for us.

We pray for our brother's safe passage to the Grand Lodge above, where we trust he will find rest and reward in the company of his fellow brethren who have gone before him.

As we say our final farewells, we offer our thanks to our brother for the guiding light he has been to us, and for the example he has set. We ask that his light continues to shine on us and help us find the way, even in the darkest moments.

We offer this prayer in the name of the Great Architect of the Universe, who guides us all. Amen.

Honoring a Life of Service

Great Architect of the Universe,

We gather together today to honor the life of our beloved brother, who has dedicated his life to service as a Freemason. We give thanks for his selfless devotion to others and his unwavering commitment to the principles of our fraternity.

As we mourn his passing, we also celebrate the legacy he leaves behind. May his life of service inspire us all to follow in his footsteps and to continue his work of making the world a better place.

We pray for comfort and strength for his family and friends, as they come to terms with their loss. May they find peace in the knowledge that our brother's service has touched countless lives and made a profound impact on the world.

We ask for your blessings on our brother's journey to the Grand Lodge above, where we trust he will find eternal rest in your loving embrace. May he be greeted by those who have gone before him, and may he find joy in the company of his fellow brethren.

As we say our final farewells, we give thanks for the many ways our brother has enriched our lives and the lives of those around us. May his legacy of service inspire us to continue his good work, and may his memory be a blessing to all who knew him.

We offer this prayer in the name of the Great Architect of the Universe, who inspires us all to lives of service and devotion. Amen.

The Heavenly Lodge

Great Architect of the Universe,

We come before you today to honor and celebrate the life of our beloved brother who has now departed from this earthly life to join the Heavenly Lodge. We are grateful for the gift of his presence in our lives, and we ask that you bless him with eternal rest and peace in your loving embrace.

As we mourn our loss, we are comforted by the knowledge that our brother has now entered into the company of the faithful departed, and is reunited with those who have gone before him. May he be welcomed with open arms, and may his spirit find joy and comfort in the Heavenly Lodge.

We pray for comfort and strength for our brother's family and friends, as they grieve his passing and seek to find solace in their memories of him. May they be consoled by the knowledge that our brother is now in a place of peace and light, and that he will be remembered forever as a faithful and devoted member of the Masonic fraternity.

As we say our final farewells, we offer our thanks for the gift of our brother's life, and for the blessings he brought to our lives. May his memory be a blessing to us all, and may we continue to honor his legacy by living lives of faith, hope, and love.

We offer this prayer in the name of the Great Architect of the Universe, who guides us all on our journey to the Heavenly Lodge. Amen.

A Life Well Lived

Great Architect of the Universe,

We gather here today to celebrate the life of our dear brother, who has left us to join the Grand Lodge above. We give thanks for the gift of his life, and for the many blessings he brought to our lives and to the lives of so many others.

Our brother lived a life that was well-lived and meaningful, filled with acts of kindness, love, and selflessness. As a Freemason, he dedicated himself to serving others, to spreading light and love, and to making the world a better place.

As we mourn his passing, we take comfort in knowing that our brother's spirit now rests in the loving embrace of the Grand Lodge above. We pray that he is surrounded by the company of those who have gone before him, and that he is filled with peace, love, and joy.

We also pray for comfort and strength for our brother's family and friends, as they come to terms with their loss. May they be comforted by the knowledge that our brother's life was one of love, faith, and service, and that he will be remembered always for his kindness, generosity, and compassion.

As we say our final farewells, we offer our thanks to you, our loving God, for the gift of our brother's life. We celebrate his legacy, and we pledge to continue his work of spreading light and love throughout the world.

We offer this prayer in the name of the Grand Architect of the Universe, who guides us on our journey of life and beyond. Amen.

The Eternal East

Great Architect of the Universe,

We come before you today to honor and celebrate the life of our beloved brother who has now passed to the Eternal East. We thank you for the gift of his presence in our lives and for the many ways in which he has touched our hearts and souls.

As a faithful member of the Masonic fraternity, our brother lived a life of service and devotion to the principles of brotherly love, relief, and truth. He was a light to all those who knew him, illuminating the path to the Eternal East and guiding us towards the mysteries of the universe.

We ask that you bless our brother with eternal rest and peace in your loving embrace. May his spirit find solace in the Celestial Lodge above, surrounded by the company of the faithful departed who have gone before him.

We also pray for comfort and strength for our brother's family and friends, as they grieve his passing and seek to find solace in their memories of him. May they be consoled by the knowledge that our brother is now in a place of peace and light, and that he will be remembered forever as a faithful and devoted member of the Masonic fraternity.

As we say our final farewells, we offer our thanks for the gift of our brother's life and for the blessings he brought to our lives. May his memory be a blessing to us all, and may we continue to honor his legacy by living lives of faith, hope, and love.

We offer this prayer in the name of the Great Architect of the Universe, who guides us all on our journey to the Eternal East. Amen.

The Celestial Lodge Eternal

Eternal and Loving Creator, Great Architect of the Universe.

We gather today to mourn the passing of our beloved brother who has now joined the Celestial Lodge above. We give thanks for the many ways in which he touched our lives and the lives of so many others, and for the legacy of kindness, compassion, and service he leaves behind.

As a faithful member of the Masonic fraternity, our brother sought to live his life in accordance with the principles of brotherly love, relief, and truth. He dedicated himself to serving others and to walking the path of enlightenment towards the Celestial Lodge above.

We pray now for his soul, that it may find eternal peace and rest in the loving embrace of the Grand Architect of the Universe. May he be surrounded by the company of the faithful departed who have gone before him, and may he be welcomed into the eternal light and love of the Celestial Lodge above.

We also pray for comfort and strength for our brother's family and friends, as they come to terms with his passing and seek to find solace in their memories of him. May they be consoled by the knowledge that our brother's spirit lives on in the love and light he brought to the world, and that he will be remembered forever as a faithful and devoted member of the Masonic fraternity.

As we say our final goodbyes, we offer our thanks for the gift of our brother's life and for the blessings he brought to our lives. May we continue to honor his memory by living lives of service, love, and devotion to the Grand Architect of the Universe.

We offer this prayer in the name of the Grand Architect of the Universe, who guides us all on our journey to the Celestial Lodge above. Amen.

A Final Salute

Great Architect of the Universe,

We come before you today to honor and pay our final respects to our dear brother who has passed from this earthly plane. He was a faithful and devoted member of the Masonic fraternity, living his life in accordance with the principles of brotherly love, relief, and truth.

We give thanks for the many ways in which he touched our lives and the lives of so many others, and for the legacy of kindness, compassion, and service he leaves behind. He was a true example of what it means to be a Mason, and we will forever remember his dedication and commitment to our shared values.

As we say our final farewell, we offer a final salute to our brother, a gesture of respect and gratitude for his faithful service to the fraternity. We ask that you bless him with eternal rest and peace in your loving embrace, and that his spirit finds solace in the Celestial Lodge above.

We also pray for comfort and strength for our brother's family and friends, as they grieve his passing and seek to find solace in their memories of him. May they be consoled by the knowledge that our brother's legacy lives on in the lives he touched and the love he shared.

As we depart from this place, we offer our thanks for the gift of our brother's life and for the blessings he brought to our lives. May we continue to honor his memory by living lives of service, love, and devotion to the Grand Architect of the Universe.

We offer this prayer in the name of the Great Architect of the Universe, who guides us all on our journey to eternal rest. Amen.

The Temple of Light

Eternal and Compassionate Creator, Great Architect of the Universe

We come before you today to honor and remember the life of our dear brother who has now passed from this world. He was a devoted leader within the Masonic fraternity, and his life was a shining example of what it means to walk in the path of brotherly love, relief, and truth.

We give thanks for the many ways in which our brother touched our lives and the lives of so many others. He was a beacon of light and inspiration, leading by example and guiding others towards the path of enlightenment.

We ask now that you welcome our brother into the Temple of Light, where he may bask in the eternal radiance of your love and wisdom. May he be surrounded by the company of the faithful departed who have gone before him, and may he find solace and comfort in the embrace of the Grand Architect of the Universe.

We also pray for comfort and strength for our brother's family and friends, as they grieve his passing and seek to find solace in their memories of him. May they be consoled by the knowledge that our brother's legacy lives on in the lives he touched and the love he shared.

As we say our final goodbyes, we offer our thanks for the gift of our brother's life and for the blessings he brought to our lives. May we continue to honor his memory by walking in the path of enlightenment and dedicating ourselves to serving others.

We offer this prayer in the name of the Grand Architect of the Universe, who guides us all on our journey to the Temple of Light. Amen.

The Journey Home

Great Architect of the Universe,

We come before you today with heavy hearts, as we mourn the passing of our dear brother who has completed his earthly journey and returned home to you. He lived a life of dedication and service to the Masonic fraternity, and his legacy will live on in the memories and hearts of all those who knew him.

As our brother journeys home to your loving embrace, we ask that you guide him with your divine light and grant him eternal peace and rest. May his spirit be welcomed into your loving presence, and may he be reunited with those who have gone before him.

We also ask for comfort and strength for our brother's family and friends, as they grieve his passing and seek to find solace in their memories of him. May they be comforted by the knowledge that our brother has completed his earthly journey and returned home to the loving arms of the Grand Architect of the Universe.

As we say our final farewells, we offer our thanks for the gift of our brother's life and for the blessings he brought to our lives. May we continue to honor his memory by living lives of service, love, and devotion to the Grand Architect of the Universe.

We offer this prayer in the name of the Great Architect of the Universe, who guides us all on our journey home. Amen.

Resting in the Arms of the Great Architect

Great Architect of the Universe,

We gather here today to honor and remember the life of our beloved brother who has now departed this earthly realm and rests in your loving arms. He was a faithful and dedicated member of the Masonic fraternity, and his life was a testament to the values of brotherhood, service, and devotion.

We give thanks for the many ways in which our brother touched our lives and the lives of those around him. He was a light in the darkness, a source of comfort and inspiration, and a true friend to all who knew him.

As our brother now rests in your loving embrace, we ask that you grant him eternal peace and rest. May he be reunited with loved ones who have gone before him, and may he bask in the radiance of your divine light.

We also ask for comfort and strength for our brother's family and friends, as they mourn his passing and seek to find solace in their memories of him. May they find comfort in the knowledge that our brother now rests in your loving arms, free from pain and suffering, and forever at peace.

As we say our final farewells, we offer our thanks for the gift of our brother's life and for the blessings he brought to our lives. May we continue to honor his memory by living lives of service, love, and devotion to the Great Architect of the Universe.

We offer this prayer in the name of the Great Architect of the Universe, who holds us all in the palm of his hand. Amen.

Honoring the Legacy

Great Architect of the Universe,

Today, we gather to honor the life and legacy of our beloved brother who has left an indelible mark on the Masonic fraternity and on the world around him. He was a man of great character, courage, and compassion, and his impact on those who knew him will never be forgotten.

We give thanks for the many ways in which our brother has enriched our lives and the lives of those around him. He lived a life of service and dedication, and his legacy will live on through the many lives he has touched and the good works he has done.

As our brother now departs this earthly realm, we ask that you grant him eternal peace and rest. May he be welcomed into your loving embrace and reunited with loved ones who have gone before him.

We also ask for comfort and strength for our brother's family and friends, as they mourn his passing and seek to find solace in their memories of him. May they be comforted by the knowledge that our brother's legacy will live on in the many lives he has touched and the good works he has done.

As we say our final farewells, we offer our thanks for the gift of our brother's life and for the blessings he brought to our lives. May we continue to honor his memory by living lives of service, love, and devotion to the Grand Architect of the Universe.

We offer this prayer in the name of the Great Architect of the Universe, who guides us all on our journey through life and beyond. Amen.

The Builder's Legacy

Great Architect of the Universe,

We gather here today to honor and remember the life of our beloved brother who was a master craftsman and a devoted member of the Masonic fraternity. He was a builder, both of physical structures and of the bonds of brotherhood and friendship, and his life was a testament to the values of excellence, hard work, and service.

We give thanks for the many ways in which our brother touched our lives and the lives of those around him. He was a teacher and a mentor, always willing to share his knowledge and expertise with those who sought to learn. He was a friend and a brother, always there to lend a hand or offer a kind word of encouragement.

As our brother now departs this earthly realm, we ask that you grant him eternal peace and rest. May he be welcomed into your loving embrace and reunited with loved ones who have gone before him.

We also ask for comfort and strength for our brother's family and friends, as they mourn his passing and seek to find solace in their memories of him. May they be comforted by the knowledge that our brother's legacy lives on in the buildings he created, the lives he touched, and the good works he did.

As we say our final farewells, we offer our thanks for the gift of our brother's life and for the blessings he brought to our lives. May we continue to honor his memory by living lives of excellence, hard work, and service, and by carrying on the great work of the Masonic fraternity.

We offer this prayer in the name of the Great Architect of the Universe, who guides us all on our journey through life and beyond. Amen.

The Compasses and Square

Great Architect of the Universe,

We gather here today to pay our final respects to our beloved brother who was a dedicated member of the Masonic fraternity. He lived his life by the principles of the Compass and Square, always seeking to do good, to live in harmony with his fellow man, and to honor the teachings of our ancient and honorable craft.

We give thanks for the many ways in which our brother enriched our lives and the lives of those around him. He was a true brother, always there to offer a kind word, a helping hand, or a listening ear. He lived a life of service, dedicating himself to the betterment of his community and the world around him.

As our brother now departs this earthly realm, we ask that you grant him eternal peace and rest. May he be welcomed into your loving embrace and reunited with loved ones who have gone before him.

We also ask for comfort and strength for our brother's family and friends, as they mourn his passing and seek to find solace in their memories of him. May they be comforted by the knowledge that our brother's legacy lives on in the good works he did, the lives he touched, and the principles he lived by.

As we say our final farewells, we offer our thanks for the gift of our brother's life and for the blessings he brought to our lives. May we continue to honor his memory by living lives of service, brotherhood, and dedication to the principles of our ancient and honorable craft.

We offer this prayer in the name of the Great Architect of the Universe, who guides us all on our journey through life and beyond. Amen.

From Darkness to Light

Great Architect of the Universe,

We gather here today to honor the memory of our departed brother who has found eternal peace in your loving embrace. We give thanks for his life, for the light he brought to the world, and for the many ways in which he touched the lives of those around him.

Our brother lived his life according to the teachings of our ancient and honorable craft, always seeking to walk in the light of your divine wisdom. He understood that the journey from darkness to light is one that we all must make, and he led by example, shining a bright light for others to follow.

As our brother now makes his journey from this earthly realm to the eternal light of your presence, we ask that you guide and comfort him on his way. May he be welcomed into your loving embrace and reunited with loved ones who have gone before him.

We also ask for comfort and strength for our brother's family and friends, as they mourn his passing and seek to find solace in the knowledge that he has found eternal peace. May they be comforted by the light of your love, and may they find strength in the memories of our brother's life and legacy.

As we say our final farewells, we offer our gratitude for the gift of our brother's life and for the light he brought to the world. May we continue to honor his memory by living lives of service, brotherhood, and dedication to the principles of our ancient and honorable craft.

We offer this prayer in the name of the Great Architect of the Universe, who guides us all on our journey from darkness to light. Amen.

The Hidden Mysteries

Great Architect of the Universe,

We gather here today to remember our beloved brother who has entered the great unknown. We give thanks for his life, for the light he brought to the world, and for the many ways in which he touched the lives of those around him.

Our brother understood that there are mysteries in this world that are beyond our understanding, and he embraced the unknown with humility and courage. He knew that the journey of life is one that we must all make, and he faced the unknown with a steadfast spirit, knowing that you were always with him.

As our brother now enters the great unknown, we ask that you guide and comfort him on his way. May he be surrounded by your love and light, and may he find rest and peace in your eternal embrace.

We also ask for comfort and strength for our brother's family and friends, as they mourn his passing and seek to find solace in the knowledge that he has found eternal peace. May they be comforted by the light of your love, and may they find strength in the memories of our brother's life and legacy.

As we say our final farewells, we offer our gratitude for the gift of our brother's life hidden for the light he brought to the world. May we continue to honor his memory by living lives of service, brotherhood, and dedication to the principles of our ancient and honorable craft.

We offer this prayer in the name of the Great Architect of the Universe, who guides us through the mysteries of life and into the great unknown. Amen.

The Trestle Board

Great Architect of the Universe,

We gather here today to honor the memory of our beloved brother who has passed from this earthly life. Our brother was a devoted Master Mason, who lived his life according to the principles of our craft and left an indelible mark on the world around him.

Our brother understood the importance of the trestle board, and he dedicated himself to building a life of meaning, purpose, and service. He lived his life according to the virtues of our craft, and he used his talents and abilities to build a better world for all.

As we remember our brother today, we give thanks for the gift of his life and for the legacy he leaves behind. May his example inspire us to continue building our own lives on the principles of our craft, and may his memory continue to guide us as we work to make a positive difference in the world.

We ask that you comfort and console our brother's family and friends during this difficult time. May they find solace in the knowledge that our brother's spirit lives on, and may they take comfort in the memories of his life and legacy.

As we say our final farewells to our brother, we ask for your guidance and support. May we continue to draw strength and inspiration from the lessons of our craft, and may we use the tools of our craft to build lives of meaning, purpose, and service.

We offer this prayer in the name of the Great Architect of the Universe, who guides us as we build our lives and our world. Amen.

The Keystone

Great Architect of the Universe,

We gather here today to mourn the passing of our faithful brother, who held our fraternity together like the keystone in an arch. Our brother lived his life as a devoted member of our fraternity, and his unwavering commitment to our craft was an inspiration to all who knew him.

Our brother understood the importance of the keystone, and he worked tirelessly to ensure that our fraternity remained strong, vibrant, and true to the principles of our craft. He was a mentor to many and a friend to all, and his love for our fraternity was evident in all that he did.

As we remember our brother today, we give thanks for the gift of his life and for the lasting impact he had on our fraternity. We are grateful for the many ways in which he held our fraternity together, and we are honored to have called him our brother.

We ask that you comfort and console our brother's family and friends during this difficult time. May they find peace in the knowledge that our brother's spirit lives on, and may they take comfort in the memories of his life and legacy.

As we say our final farewells to our brother, we ask for your guidance and support. May we continue to draw strength and inspiration from his example, and may we work to honor his legacy by holding our fraternity together with the same unwavering commitment and dedication that he showed us.

We offer this prayer in the name of the Great Architect of the Universe, who guides us as we strive to live our lives according to the principles of our craft. Amen.

Final Farewell

Dear Great Architect of the Universe,

We gather here today to bid farewell to our dear brother/sister who has passed on from this world. As Freemasons, we understand that death is an inevitable part of life, and we believe that our brother/sister has now entered into your eternal presence.

We take comfort in knowing that they lived a life guided by the principles of our fraternity: brotherly love, relief, and truth. They embodied the virtues of charity, kindness, and generosity, and their presence in our lodge will be sorely missed.

We ask that you grant our brother/sister peace and comfort in your heavenly kingdom, where they may continue to live a life guided by the values of Freemasonry. We also ask that you comfort their family and loved ones during this difficult time, and that you grant them the strength to carry on in the wake of this loss.

We give thanks for the life of our brother/sister, and for the light that they brought into our lives. May they rest in peace, and may their memory be a blessing to all who knew them.

We offer this prayer in the name of the Great Architect of the Universe. Amen

Invocation of Gratitude

Great Architect of the Universe,

We come before you today with heavy hearts as we gather to honor the life and legacy of our dear friend and brother who has recently passed away. We give thanks for the life that was lived, for the memories we shared, and for the impact that our beloved brother had on the lives of so many.

Our brother lived his life as a true Freemason, embodying the principles of brotherly love, relief, and truth in all that he did. He was a man of great integrity and honor, who always put the needs of others before his own. His commitment to living a life of service and compassion was evident in everything he did, from his work within the Masonic community to his contributions to his local community and beyond.

As we gather to mourn his passing, we find comfort in the knowledge that our brother's spirit lives on in the hearts of all those he touched. He was a beacon of light in a world that can often be dark and difficult, and his legacy will continue to inspire and guide us for years to come.

We remember with gratitude the many ways in which our brother gave of himself. He was always willing to lend a helping hand to those in need, to offer a kind word of encouragement, or to simply be a listening ear to those who needed someone to talk to. His generosity of spirit knew no bounds, and he touched the lives of so many people in such meaningful ways.

Our brother was deeply committed to the Masonic principles of brotherly love, relief, and truth. He believed in the power of these principles to transform lives, and he dedicated his life to living them out in his daily interactions with others. He was a mentor to many, always willing to share his wisdom and experience with those who were just starting on their own Masonic journeys.

As we bid our brother farewell, we pray that you will grant him eternal rest and peace in your loving embrace. We pray that he will find comfort and joy in the company of all those who have gone before him, and that he will be reunited with those he loved and cherished in this life.

We also ask for your guidance and wisdom as we continue to honor our brother's memory and carry on the work that he began. May we be inspired by his example to continue to live lives of service and compassion, always seeking to make a positive difference in the world around us.

We offer this prayer in deepest gratitude for the life of our dear friend and brother, and in reverence to the Great Architect of the Universe, who has called him home.

Amen

The Royal Arch

Great Architect of the Universe,

We gather here today to remember and honor our respected companion and brother who has passed from this mortal life. Our brother lived his life as a true companion, and his contributions to our Royal Arch community were invaluable.

Our brother understood the significance of the Royal Arch, and he worked tirelessly to promote and preserve the traditions and values of our organization. He was a dedicated companion who mentored and inspired countless others, leaving a lasting impact on our fraternity.

As we remember our brother today, we give thanks for the gift of his life and for his many contributions to our fraternity. We are grateful for the many ways in which he served and led, and we are honored to have called him our companion and brother.

We ask that you comfort and console our brother's family and friends during this difficult time. May they find solace in the memories of our brother's life and legacy, and may they take comfort in the knowledge that his spirit lives on.

As we say our final farewells to our brother, we ask for your guidance and support. May we continue to draw inspiration from his example of service and dedication, and may we work to honor his memory by living our lives according to the principles of our Royal Arch community.

We offer this prayer in the name of the Great Architect of the Universe, who guides us as we strive to live our lives in service to our fellow companions and brothers. Amen.

The Apron of Honor

Great Architect of the Universe,

We gather here today to honor and remember our dedicated brother who has passed on from this mortal life. Our brother lived a life of service and devotion, and his commitment to the principles of our fraternity was unwavering.

As we come together to pay our respects to our brother, we are reminded of the significance of the apron of honor. Our brother wore his apron with pride and distinction, embodying the values of our fraternity and serving as an inspiration to all who knew him.

We are grateful for the gift of our brother's life and for the many ways in which he served and supported our fraternity. His contributions to our community will not be forgotten, and we will strive to honor his legacy by continuing to live according to the principles of our fraternity.

We ask that you comfort and console our brother's family and friends during this difficult time. May they find solace in the memories of our brother's life and legacy, and may they take comfort in the knowledge that his spirit lives on.

As we say our final farewells to our brother, we ask for your guidance and support. May we continue to draw inspiration from his example of service and dedication, and may we work to honor his memory by living our lives according to the principles of our fraternity.

We offer this prayer in the name of the Great Architect of the Universe, who guides us as we strive to live our lives in service to others.

Amen

The Working Tools

Great Architect of the Universe,

We gather here today to pay our respects to our skilled craftsman and devoted brother who has passed on from this mortal life. Our brother was a master of his craft and a true embodiment of the values of our fraternity.

As we come together to honor and remember our brother, we are reminded of the significance of the working tools. Our brother was a master of his craft, using his skill and dedication to create works of art that will stand the test of time.

We are grateful for the gift of our brother's life and for the many ways in which he shared his talent and skill with others. His contributions to our fraternity and our community will not be forgotten, and we will strive to honor his legacy by continuing to use our own working tools to create a better world.

We ask that you comfort and console our brother's family and friends during this difficult time. May they find solace in the memories of our brother's life and legacy, and may they take comfort in the knowledge that his spirit lives on.

As we say our final farewells to our brother, we ask for your guidance and support. May we continue to draw inspiration from his example of skill and dedication, and may we work to honor his memory by using our own working tools to create a better world.

We offer this prayer in the name of the Great Architect of the Universe, who guides us as we strive to live our lives in service to others.

Amen

The Traveling Man

Great Architect of the Universe,

We come before you today to honor the memory of our beloved brother who has walked the straight and narrow path of righteousness. Our brother lived a life of honor, integrity, and devotion to the teachings of our fraternity.

We give thanks for the life of our brother, who embodied the values of the square and compasses. He was a man of great character, whose unwavering commitment to truth, justice, and morality inspired all who knew him.

As we gather to say our final goodbyes to our brother, we ask that you guide and comfort his family and loved ones. May they find strength and solace in the knowledge that our brother's legacy will live on through the countless lives he touched during his time with us.

We also ask that you bless our brother with eternal rest and peace. May he find joy and fulfillment in your loving embrace, and may he be reunited with all those who have gone before him.

We offer this prayer in the name of the Great Architect of the Universe, who has guided our brother throughout his life and will continue to guide us as we strive to live our lives in accordance with the principles of the square and compasses. Amen.

The Perfect Ashlar

Great Architect of the Universe,

Today we gather to celebrate the life of our beloved brother who has reached the height of his virtue and become the perfect ashlar. Our brother lived a life of dedication to the principles of our fraternity, and his steadfast commitment to virtue and morality inspired all who knew him.

As we say our final goodbyes to our brother, we ask that you guide and comfort his family and loved ones. May they find solace in the knowledge that our brother has reached the pinnacle of his journey and has found eternal rest and peace in your loving embrace.

We give thanks for our brother's life, and for the many ways in which he has touched the lives of those around him. May his legacy live on through the countless lives he has influenced and inspired, and may his memory be a source of strength and inspiration to us all.

We also ask that you bless our brother with eternal rest and peace. May he find joy and fulfillment in your presence, and may he be reunited with all those who have gone before him.

We offer this prayer in the name of the Great Architect of the Universe, who has guided our brother throughout his life and will continue to guide us as on our journeys as we strive to live our lives in accordance with the principles of the perfect ashlar. Amen.

The Mystic Tie

Great Architect of the Universe, we gather here today to honor the memory of our departed brother who has passed from this earthly plane to the eternal realm of the spirit. We thank you for the life of this beloved brother, who dedicated himself to the principles of our great Fraternity.

As we mourn his passing, we take comfort in the knowledge that the Mystic Tie that binds us all as Freemasons remains unbroken, and that our brother remains bound to us in spirit. May his passing remind us of the fragility of life, and of the importance of cherishing the bonds of friendship and brotherhood that unite us all.

We pray that our brother's soul may find peace and rest in your loving arms, and that he may continue to guide and inspire us in the years to come. May his legacy of wisdom, strength, and compassion continue to be a guiding light for all those who follow in his footsteps.

We offer this prayer in gratitude for the life of our brother, and in the hope that we may all continue to walk the path of the mystic tie with honor, dignity, and grace.

Amen

The Great Architect's Design

Great Architect of the Universe, we gather here today to honor the memory of our departed brother, who has left an indelible mark on our fraternity's history.

We are grateful for the time we shared with him and for the wisdom and guidance he imparted during his life. He was a true craftsman, who always sought to perfect his work, both in the lodge and in his personal life.

We find comfort in knowing that he has now completed his earthly journey and has joined you in your eternal abode. We pray that you embrace him in your loving arms and guide him to the celestial lodge above, where he may continue his work in the service of your divine plan.

As we bid him farewell, we celebrate his life and the impact he had on all those who knew him. May his memory be a source of inspiration for us to continue to strive for excellence in all that we do.

We ask that you grant his family and loved ones the strength to bear the loss and the comfort of knowing that he now rests in your perfect design. We also pray for the fraternity, that we may continue to uphold the values and principles that he held dear.

In your infinite wisdom and mercy, we commend our brother to your care, confident that he has found peace and eternal rest in your loving embrace. Amen.

The Lost Word

Great Architect of the Universe, we gather today to honor the life and mourn the passing of our beloved Brother who has returned to the divine source. As Freemasons, we understand that death is not an end but a new beginning, a transformation of the spirit into a higher state of being. Our Brother has now completed his earthly journey, and we trust that he has found peace and comfort in the arms of the Grand Master of the Universe.

We are reminded of the symbol of the Lost Word, the great mystery of our Craft that our Brother now knows the answer to. May his journey to the Celestial Lodge Above be filled with light, and may he find everlasting joy in the company of those who have gone before him.

As we say our final farewell to our Brother, we also celebrate his life and his contribution to our Fraternity. He lived his life by the principles of our Craft, spreading kindness, brotherly love, and charity. He was a dedicated Mason who embodied the true meaning of our symbols and teachings.

We thank you, Great Architect of the Universe, for the time we shared with our Brother, and we pray that his memory will remain forever in our hearts. May we continue to honor his legacy by living our lives in accordance with the teachings of our Fraternity, and by always striving to make the world a better place. Amen.

The Widow's Son

Great Architect of the Universe,

We gather here today to honor the memory of our beloved Brother who has passed from this earthly plane. He was a devoted Freemason, who always lived by the principles of our Order. He embodied the values of charity, compassion, and selflessness that are at the heart of our fraternity.

We remember his life with gratitude and appreciation, for he was a true example of the Widow's Son. He was always ready to help those in need, and he gave of himself freely and without reservation. He lived a life of service, always putting the needs of others before his own.

We pray that he has found eternal rest in the Divine Source, where he is reunited with his loved ones who have gone before him. May he continue to inspire us with his example of charity and compassion, and may we honor his legacy by following in his footsteps.

As we say our final farewell to our Brother, we ask that you guide his soul on his journey to the Celestial Lodge above. We pray that he may find peace and joy in your eternal embrace.

Rest in peace, dear Brother. You will always be remembered with love and respect. Amen.

The Acacia

Great Architect of the Universe,

We gather here today to pay our respects and bid farewell to our beloved brother who has passed from this earthly plane to the next. We mourn his loss, but we also celebrate his life and the legacy he has left behind.

As we stand here in this solemn moment, we cannot help but be reminded of the Acacia, the symbol of our fraternity's eternal life. Just as the Acacia is an emblem of immortality, our brother's life and work will continue to flourish and bear fruit long after he is gone.

He embodied the virtues of charity and compassion, always extending a helping hand to those in need. He was a true brother to all, offering comfort and support in times of joy and sorrow. He worked tirelessly to strengthen our fraternity, and his dedication and leadership will be sorely missed.

But we take comfort in knowing that his spirit lives on in the hearts and minds of all those he touched. We remember his kind words, his selfless deeds, and the warmth of his friendship. He has left an indelible mark on our fraternity and on all those who knew him.

Great Architect of the Universe, we ask that you welcome our brother into your loving embrace. May he rest in peace, and may his memory be a blessing to us all. Amen.